First Facts®

The Solar System

The First Moon Landing

by Steve Kortenkamp

Consultant:
James Gerard
Aerospace Education Specialist, NASA
Kennedy Space Center, Florida

Capstone *press*®

Mankato, Minnesota

First Facts is published by Capstone Press,
151 Good Counsel Drive, P.O. Box 669, Mankato, Minnesota 56002.
www.capstonepress.com

Library of Congress Cataloging-in-Publication Data
Kortenkamp, Steve.
  The first moon landing / by Steve Kortenkamp.
    p. cm.—(First facts. The solar system)
  Summary: "Describes the first landing on the moon, including information about the space
race and the Apollo 11 crew and spacecraft"—Provided by publisher.
  Includes bibliographical references and index.
  ISBN-13: 978-1-4296-0060-6 (hardcover)
  ISBN-10: 1-4296-0060-8 (hardcover)
  1. Project Apollo (U.S.)—Juvenile literature. 2. Apollo 11 (Spacecraft)—Juvenile literature.
3. Space flight to the moon—Juvenile literature. I. Title. II. Series.
TL789.8.U6A5434 2008
629.45'4—dc22   2006100045

Editorial Credits
Jennifer Besel, editor; Juliette Peters, set designer; Patrick Dentinger, book designer; Jo Miller,
    photo researcher

Photo Credits
Getty Images Inc./Hulton Archive, 6
McDonald Observatory, 20 (right)
NASA, cover, 1, 4–5, 10–11, 13, 16, 19, 21; Johnson Space Center, 9, 20 (left); Michael Collins, 15;
    Neil A. Armstrong, 17
ZUMA Press/KPA, 14

1 2 3 4 5 6 12 11 10 09 08 07

Table of Contents

Dreaming of the Moon

People have always gazed up and wondered what it would be like to stand on the Moon. In 1969, two men stood on the Moon for the first time. And in doing so, they helped the United States win a race.

the Russian satellite, *Sputnik*, launching into space

The Space Race

In the 1950s and 1960s, the United States was in a **cold war** with the **Soviet Union**. When the Soviet Union launched the first **satellite**, the United States wanted to do something better. The space race had begun. Each country wanted to be the first to send people to the Moon.

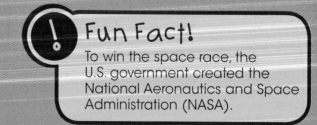

Fun Fact!
To win the space race, the U.S. government created the National Aeronautics and Space Administration (NASA).

Practice Makes Perfect

Getting to the Moon wasn't easy. Before going to the Moon, astronauts had to do test flights. They learned how to launch the rocket and circle Earth. Then they sent astronauts on a test flight to circle the Moon and return to Earth.

 Fun Fact!
Astronauts trained on flight simulators. These machines helped them learn how to control the spacecraft they would use to land on the Moon.

Apollo 11

The first **mission** sent to land on the Moon was *Apollo 11*. Neil Armstrong was the commander of the mission. Buzz Aldrin and Michael Collins were the pilots. Armstrong and Aldrin were chosen to be the first people to walk on the Moon.

Fun Fact!
The crew of *Apollo 11* had trained as astronauts for more than five years.

Going to the Moon

On July 16, 1969, *Apollo 11* was sent into space. First, the astronauts circled Earth. Then they fired another rocket that sent them to the Moon. The trip took three days.

The *Apollo 11* spacecraft had two parts. The astronauts traveled in the command **module**. The lunar module was used to land on the Moon.

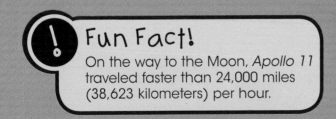

! Fun Fact!
On the way to the Moon, *Apollo 11* traveled faster than 24,000 miles (38,623 kilometers) per hour.

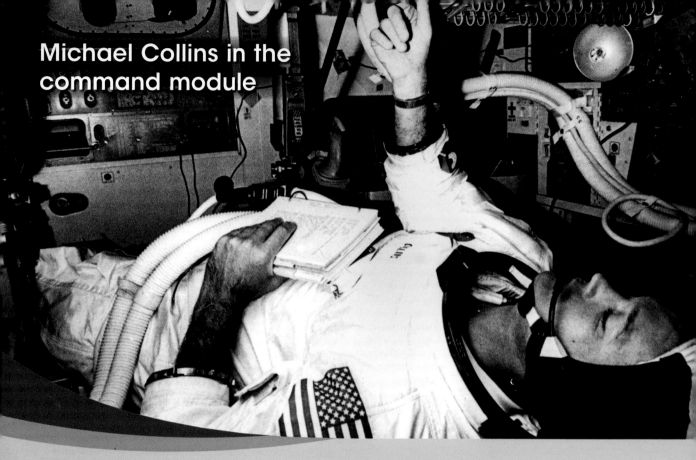

Michael Collins in the command module

Landing on the Moon

When *Apollo 11* got near the Moon, Armstrong and Aldrin climbed through a tunnel into the lunar module. Collins stayed behind in the command module.

Armstrong fired the rockets on the lunar module. He pulled away from the command module and made a soft landing on the Moon on July 20, 1969.

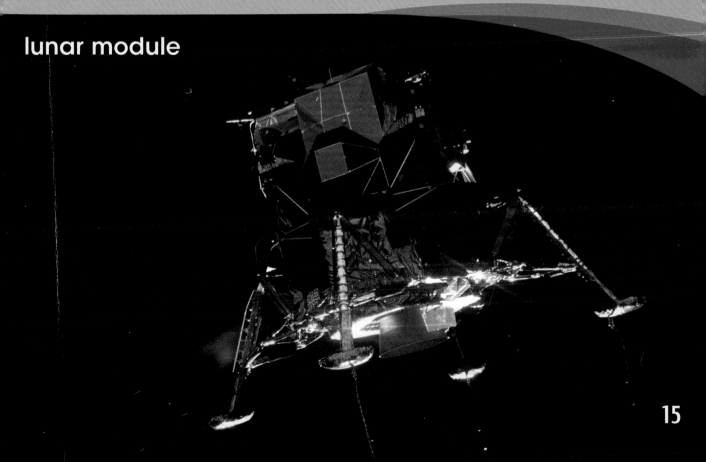

lunar module

Exploring the Moon

Millions of people watched on TV as Armstrong took the first step onto the Moon. He said, "That's one small step for a man, one giant leap for mankind."

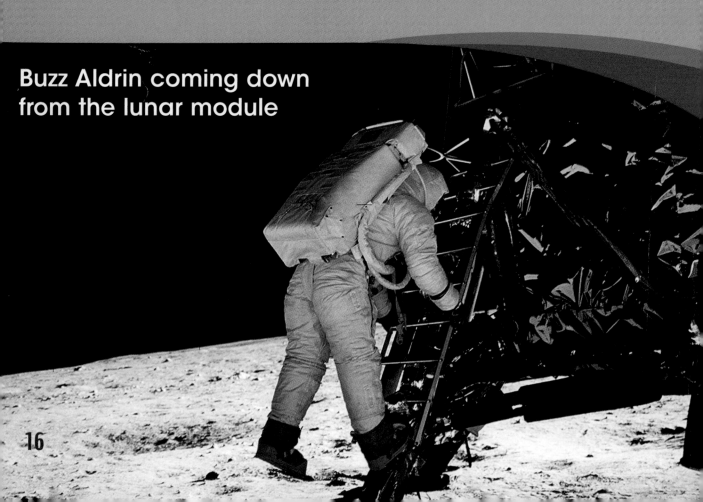

Buzz Aldrin coming down from the lunar module

Aldrin followed Armstrong onto the Moon. They collected rocks. They also set up **experiments** so scientists on Earth could study the Moon.

Coming Home

After a day on the Moon, Armstrong and Aldrin rejoined the command module in space. Collins fired the spacecraft's rockets to send them home.

When they reached Earth, parachutes slowed them to a gentle splashdown in the ocean. The crew was safe. The United States won the space race.

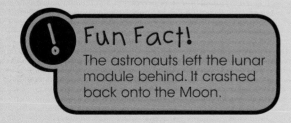

! Fun Fact!
The astronauts left the lunar module behind. It crashed back onto the Moon.

Armstrong and Aldrin left experiments on the Moon. One is an instrument that reflects laser beams. Scientists on Earth shoot lasers at the instrument to measure the distance to the Moon. They have discovered that the Moon moves about 1 inch (2.5 centimeters) farther away from Earth each year.

Think Big!

Today, scientists study the Moon with robot spacecraft. They have discovered places on the Moon that might have a lot of ice. Now the United States is planning to send astronauts back to the Moon. They can use the ice to make rocket fuel and oxygen to breathe. What are some other ways astronauts could use the ice to help them live on the Moon?

Glossary

cold war (KOHLD WOR)—a conflict between the United States and the Soviet Union; although there was no direct fighting, the conflict lasted from about 1947 to 1990.

experiment (ek-SPER-uh-ment)—a scientific test to find out how something works

mission (MISH-uhn)—a planned job or task

module (MOJ-ool)—a separate section that can be joined to other parts

satellite (SAT-uh-lite)—a spacecraft that circles Earth; satellites take pictures and send messages to Earth.

Soviet Union (SOH-vee-et YOON-yuhn)—a former group of 15 republics that included Russia, Ukraine, and other nations in eastern Europe and northern Asia

Read More

Adamson, Thomas K. *The First Moon Landing*. Graphic History. Mankato, Minn.: Capstone Press, 2007.

Crewe, Sabrina, and Dale Anderson. *The First Moon Landing*. Events That Shaped America. Milwaukee: Gareth Stevens, 2004.

Koestler-Grack, Rachel A. *Moon Landing*. American Moments. Edina, Minn.: Abdo, 2005.

Internet Sites

FactHound offers a safe, fun way to find Internet sites related to this book. All of the sites on FactHound have been researched by our staff.

Here's how:
1. Visit *www.facthound.com*
2. Choose your grade level.
3. Type in this book ID **1429600608** for age-appropriate sites. You may also browse subjects by clicking on letters, or by clicking on pictures and words.
4. Click on the **Fetch It** button.

Facthound will fetch the best sites for you!

Index